THIS BOOK
BELONGS TO

....

MINECRAFT SECRETS & CHEATS: ANNUAL 2020
A CENTUM BOOK 978-1-913110-82-6
Published in Great Britain by Centum Books Ltd
This edition published 2019

1 3 5 7 9 10 8 6 4 2

Centum Books Ltd, 20 Devon Square, Newton Abbot, Devon, TQ12 2HR, UK
books@centumbooksltd.co.uk

CENTUM BOOKS Limited Reg. No. 07641486

A CIP catalogue record for this book is available from the British Library.

Printed in Italy.

centum

MINECRAFT
SECRETS & CHEATS
ANNUAL
2020

CONTENTS

WHAT'S INSIDE?!

THINGS TO FIND

Loads of ideas on pages 10, 34 and 54!

20 AMAZING BUILD IDEAS!
GET INSPIRATION HERE!

LOADS OF MINECRAFT PUZZLES!
Test your brain on pages 14, 24, 30 and 48!

52 HEROBRINE!
HAVE YOU SEEN HIM?!

PLUS

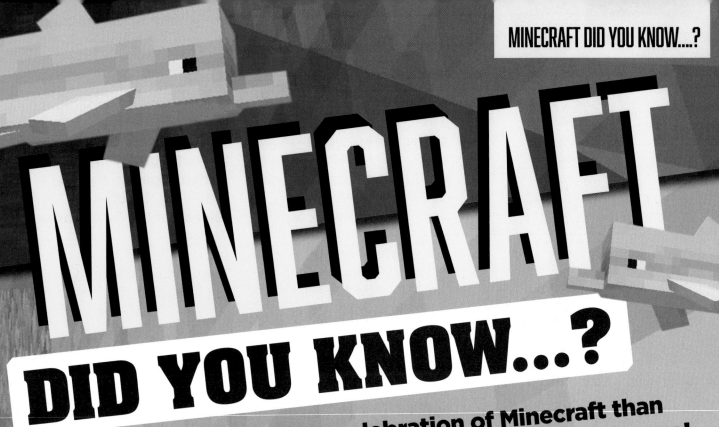

MINECRAFT DID YOU KNOW...?

What better way to start our celebration of Minecraft than with a collection of amazing facts about our favourite game!

The first official release of Minecraft was in late 2011, although early test versions were available a year or two before that. The game looked a little different back then and has regularly evolved through ongoing updates!

The first test version of Minecraft took under a week to make! Back then, it was called Cave Game, before its name changed to Minecraft: Order Of The Stone. And then, of course, to Minecraft!

The world record for the most time spent playing Minecraft was set by Mark Walls-Sawchuk. In June 2016, he played the game non-stop for 35 hours, 40 minutes and two seconds. He was raising money for charity (but was allowed toilet breaks!).

The original creator of Minecraft, Notch, used social media to see if anyone wanted to buy his company and the game when he'd had enough of working on it. Microsoft – makers of the Xbox consoles – paid him over two billion dollars just three months later!

If you want to understand what an enderman is saying, it's just English, but backwards! The noise of a ghast, meanwhile, is made by a cat!

At the end of 2018, the only video game to have sold more copies than

There's a Minecraft film in the works, although it's not expected until 2021 at the earliest. The producer of *The LEGO Movie* is working on the project, which is going to be released by Warner Bros (the studio behind the *Harry Potter* films!).

Minecraft spin-off games have been produced! Minecraft: Story Mode was the first, a series of adventures released across two seasons in the visual style of Minecraft. There was even a version you could play using Netflix as well! The second spin-off is the newer Minecraft Dungeons game, which can be played by up to four people.

Lots of schools use Minecraft! So much so that a special Education Edition of the game was made and is now available around the world.

Minecraft was a hit very quickly, and without having to spend money on advertising! It soon notched up one million sales in a few weeks (and that was just for the beta version)! People found out about the game by other people talking about it and recommending it. That word of mouth got stronger up to and following the official release of the first proper version.

The original default skin in Minecraft

was that of Steve. But in 2014, Mojang added Alex as well. Since then, you've been able to start a game as either character, one male, one female.

Minecraft is Tetris. And that's been around since the 1980s! In all, over 150 million copies of Minecraft have been bought around the world.

Minecraft has been released on lots of formats, but not all of them are supported any more. Whilst you can play the game on the PlayStation 3, the PS Vita, the Xbox 360 and Nintendo WiiU, you can't get updates for those versions of the game any more. Nor can you get updates for the Apple TV and Raspberry Pi versions any more!

The most popular version of Minecraft is the Pocket Edition played on tablets and mobile phones.

There have been spin-off novels from the Minecraft world that have been officially endorsed by Mojang! Authors such as Max Brooks and Tracey Baptiste have written adventures like *The Island* and *The Crash*, which each take place in the Minecraft world!

Official Minecraft LEGO sets were first made available in 2012 after someone submitted the idea to LEGO at the end of 2011. There was enough interest and the idea was approved. The first set arrived later on in 2012.

Minecraft makes an appearance in the movie *Ready Player One*, which came out in 2018! In the film's opening scenes, you can clearly see a Minecraft planet. The game has also popped up in the likes of *The Simpsons* and an assortment of other videogames too!

The first ever MineCon official Minecraft convention was held in November 2011 in Las Vegas, USA. Can you believe they only had 4500 tickets available?! They were all snapped up by the end of October! The following year's MineCon was held at Disneyland Paris, and they've been an annual event since, moving online back in 2017 so that we could all watch, whether we had a ticket or not!

The actual size of blocks in the game is supposed to relate to real life. Well, sort of! One block is said to represent one metre cubed in the real world.

The problem with that is it would mean a chicken was, well, three feet tall! Nearly twice as tall as the average human. Yikes!

Some features get taken away from Minecraft over time. For instance, biomes such as Seasonal Forest, Shrubland and Tundra have been removed from the game. Even some of the sounds in the game have changed over time as Minecraft has evolved and improved more and more.

There are no plans at all for a separate Minecraft 2, although the question does come up from time to time. Instead, Mojang is focusing on continual updates to Minecraft. It tends to announce some of its biggest updates at each winter's MineCon convention.

SCAVENGER HUNT PART 1

It's Part 1 of our Minecraft scavenger hunt. Can you track down and take a screenshot of EVERYTHING on our list? Challenge your friends to see who can get the most!

There are 101 items to find spread across the annual – here are the first 34! Remember, everything has to be NATURALLY generated – stuff you craft or place doesn't count!

A desert well

Watch out for the patrol!

A flower forest

EASY STUFF

1 point each

1 A desert well
2 Some mushrooms growing underground
3 A patrol of pillagers
4 A wild pumpkin patch
5 A flower forest
6 A full moon
7 A forest fire started by lava
8 A grass path
9 Sand that's ready to fall if you touch it
10 Water (or lava) dripping through the rocks above

LANDSCAPE FEATURES

5 points each

11 A lagoon on the coastline

12 A dust bowl where the soil has been stripped away on the side of a mountain

13 A cave that leads all the way through a mountain and out the other side

14 A mountain that rises above the clouds

15 A ravine that intersects with another ravine

16 An island with a single tree on it

17 A cave with a river flowing down it

18 A river that has mostly dried up

A cave river

Mountain above the clouds

An island with one tree

A surface mine

Zombies destroy turtle eggs

The rarest biome

RARE STUFF

19 A zombie wearing gold armour
20 Flowers growing in the entrance of an abandoned mine
21 A gold mine above ground in a Mesa biome
22 A dolphin swimming in a river
23 A village on the edge of a coastline
24 Zombies destroying turtle eggs
25 Some emerald ore
26 A Mushroom Island biome

GLITCHES

20 points each

27 A witch hut with extremely long legs

28 An igloo basement with broken walls

29 A chunk of land floating unsupported in the sky

30 A house on the side of a hill

31 A desert temple where the door is buried

32 A jungle temple in the middle of a lake

33 An abandoned mine that intersects another mine

34 A shipwreck that's completely out of the water

A tall witch hut

A block floating unsupported

A glitch village

PUZZLE PAGES

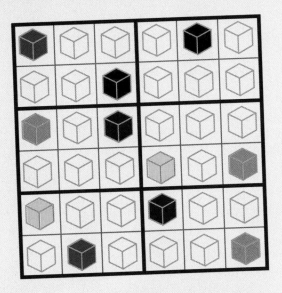
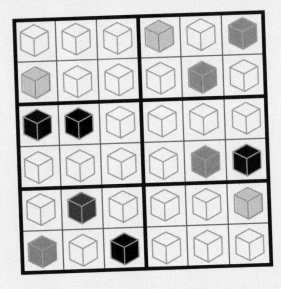
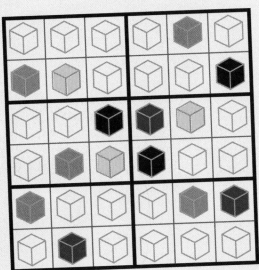
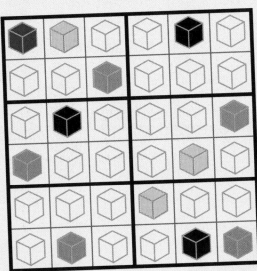

BLOCKDOKU

 Iron Red Sandstone Ice Obsidian Emerald Gold

Can you colour in the block grids above following three simple rules?
1) Each square must contain a block
2) Each of the red rectangles must contain all six kinds of block
3) No type of block can appear on any line twice, horizontally or vertically

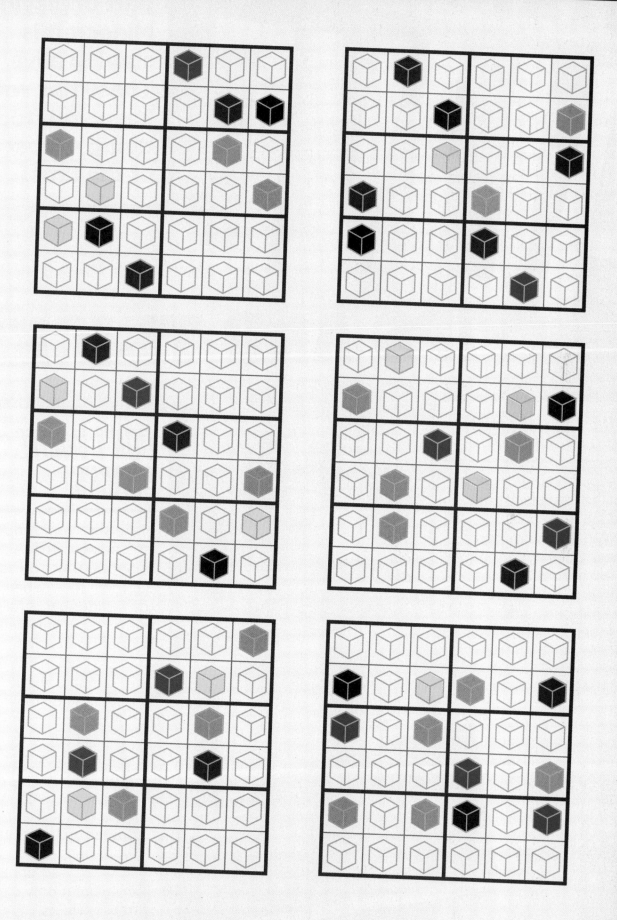

STAYING ALIVE TIPS AND TRICKS

The hardest part of playing Minecraft is staying alive. These tips will keep you from dying – most of the time!

FILL UP ON FOOD

Keeping your hunger bar full will replenish your health and allow you to run, so always carry food. Cake and rabbit stew restore the most items, but cake has low saturation so your hunger will start dropping again soon after eating it, and rabbit stew takes a lot of crafting.

Cooked steak and porkchops are the best food sources. They restore 8 points of health and 12.8 points of saturation, and they stack in the inventory, so you can carry plenty!

Cake is good!

Eat an enchanted golden apple for special effects

DON'T WASTE SNACKS

Make sure your food isn't being eaten unnecessarily. You can't eat most food when the hunger bar is full, but if you're only half a hunger point down, eat a cookie rather than a whole cooked steak! The two foods you CAN eat when full are chorus fruit and golden apples, because they have beneficial effects other than restoring your hunger bar. You can also drink milk, but it only clears status effects.

GET A HORSE (OR A BOAT)

The easiest way to put yourself in danger is to lower your hunger bar by sprinting. But walking is very slow, and mobs are almost as quick as you when you're not running. The way to get around this is to travel using an alternative method! Horses (and horse variants) are perfect for crossing long distances easily, and while they can't swim, you can (and should!) cross water using a boat instead.

Ride a horse

FIGHT DIRTY

The best defence is a good offence, so make sure you dispatch your enemies as quickly as possible. Critical hits do extra damage over a normal blow, so use them whenever you can. To do a critical hit with a sword or axe, jump and strike your enemy as you land. To do one with a bow, pull back the arrow as far as possible before releasing it. As you build experience, enchant your weapons for extra slaying power!

Land critical hits

STOCK UP

The most common blocks in the game are cobblestone, wood planks and iron ingots, which together appear in around 100 different crafting recipes. With these three items, you can make all of the essential recipes, from furnaces to crafting tables to tools, weapons and armour. Don't leave home without a stack of each one in your inventory, and you'll be ready for almost anything!

DON'T GET GREEDY

Hunting for resources is great fun, but the further you travel from your base, the deadlier things become. If you're collecting rare ore or stocking up on wood, drop it off somewhere safe at regular intervals. The longer your journey, the more chance you have of starving or weakening too much to go on – and then losing it all if you die!

Store valuable inventory regularly

LISTEN OUT

It's easy to focus on the stuff you can see around you, but don't forget to keep your ears open too, especially when you're underground. Listening to sounds around you is the perfect way to navigate away from danger. A zombie's moan, a skeleton's bony clink or the hiss of a creeper can all tell you danger's around, while bubbling lava or running water let you know there's a cavern – and some potential riches – close by!

DRESS FOR THE OCCASION

Always wear the best armour you can. Once you have an iron pickaxe, get some iron armour. Once you start finding diamonds, save them for diamond armour. You can't die if you can't be hurt, and wearing the strongest possible armour will take care of it. Leather armour is just for decoration – by the time you can even find enough leather to craft it, you should be well on your way to smelting ingots!

Wear the best armour

ALWAYS LOOK DOWN

Fall damage is the hardest type of damage to protect yourself against, and there's almost no way to guard against it altogether. If you have to make a long drop, aim to land in some water to avoid damage completely, while landing on a bed, hay bale or slime block will also reduce damage. What you should really do is use the sneak key near a ledge, as you can't fall while you're sneaking!

Sneak and you won't fall in

KEEP IT LIGHT

Light levels matter – a lot. Light keeps hostile mobs from spawning and draws in friendly mobs, whereas the dark can hide all manner of evil creatures who are just waiting to separate you from your long-term plans. You can never have too many torches, so place them frequently and often. They don't just keep evil mobs away, they're also handy if you want to find your way back from a long journey once night falls!

Light everywhere you can!

DON'T GET INTO A FIGHT

Staying out of fights you can't win is key to long-term survival. Skill aside, fights don't become easier the more you win them. The best way to deal with this? Don't get into fights at all. This might sound obvious, but it's easy to be too confident once you've won a few. If you see three creepers in a tight space, the best way to stay alive is to get out tif there as quickly as possible. You can always kill them another day!

25 BUILD IDEAS

Stuck for what to build? Here are a few prompts to get your creative juices flowing!

2 PARK

The wild landscape of Minecraft is impressive in its own way, but why not flatten out some land and manicure it into your own quaint-looking park? Plant trees and flowers, build a duck pond and, of course, surround it with railings.

1 GOLD MINE

Why not make yourself a mine? You can find abandoned mines around the world, but rarely on the surface. Build yourself a cool minecart system, and fill it with rare ore!

3 FAST FOOD RESTAURANT

Why not build your own fast food restaurant – McMinecraft's?! Fill it with seating, add a counter, and you'll be flipping burgers in no time!

4 MONORAIL

It's not TECHNICALLY a monorail because everything in Minecraft has two rails, but an elevated train system built from minecarts will give you a quick way to travel with a fantastic view!

SHOP

5

Why not build a bakery or a fishmongers? Large glass windows, a till and some display racks are all easy to make in Minecraft.

SECRET BASE

9

Whether you make a secret high-tech basement accessed by a hatch or a hollowed-out hideaway in a mountain, there's no base better than the supervillain's choice – a secret base!

WATERWHEEL

6

Alternatively, if you want to keep things rural, find a tranquil river and add a waterwheel-powered mill at the water's edge. Build it out of wood for an authentic look.

GARDEN

10

What's a house without a garden? Surround it with bushes or a fence, add a patio and furniture, or a rustic bench and water feature – either way, you'll have the perfect place to relax outdoors.

BRIDGE

7

Sick of swimming awkwardly across rivers or hiking around lakes? An old-fashioned bridge – or a modern one! – is a great project to help you really put your stamp on the world.

FARM

11

Minecraft's typical farms are small and basic. Why not build a full-size one with a barn, farmhouse, fields of wheat and, of course, a field full of cattle? Ah, the simple life!

SWIMMING POOL

8

You can swim in the lakes, rivers and sea, but nothing beats your own pool. Line it with prismarine, light it with sea lanterns, and add your own diving board and Jacuzzi.

12 NETHER BASE

The Nether is an unforgiving place, so why not build your own safe haven there around your entry portal? It will make coming and going far, far less stressful!

HENGE 15

Just as the Druids built Stonehenge, you can build your own henge in Minecraft to give an ancient, historical feel to your world. Add a portal or enchanting table for a mystical touch!

WATER PARK 13

Nothing beats a water park for fun. Build water spouts, slides, boat races, a diving area and more to bring some water-world fun to Minecraft.

16 TREEHOUSE

Living on the ground is fine, but up in the trees is perhaps the safest place. No mobs are going to climb all the way up there without you spotting them!

ROLLERCOASTER 17

Life may be a rollercoaster, but an ACTUAL rollercoaster is a much better one. Use tracks and redstone-powered rails to speed a cart around your own twisty, turn-y track.

14 LIGHTHOUSE

Why are there so many shipwrecks in Minecraft? Probably because there are no lighthouses! Fix that by building some using redstone lamps and daylight sensors to automate them!

18 VOLCANO

Minecraft has plenty of mountains and lava but no volcanoes. Dig a crater in a hill, then combine it with a lava source and magma blocks for an active volcano look!

19 PIXELART CREATION

Minecraft's coloured blocks make the perfect palette for some pixelart, so why not stack them up to make your own creation based on Pokémon, Mario, or anything you like?

23 MAP WALL

Mapping large areas in Minecraft is fun, but why not display your maps as one huge map by filling a wall with item frames and placing the maps inside them so they join up?

20 A MODERN HOUSE

Fancy yourself as an architect? Why not design your perfect two (three, or four!) bedroom home? Furnishing each room in a way that looks real is a great little puzzle in itself!

24 THEME PARK

Want to entertain your friends? Why not build a theme park based around your favourite pop-culture icons? Make it a Minecraft-centric experience with escape rooms, mazes, jumping puzzles and more!

21 ZOO

Want to see all of Minecraft's animals in one place? Then it's up to you to house them. Build their habitats and populate your zoo with animals for people to come and visit. Don't forget to feed them!

25 JUNGLE PYRAMID

Clear out the jungle and use carved stone blocks to put up a Mayan-style stepped pyramid. Cover it with vines for an overgrown look, and don't forget the skeletons and treasure inside!

22 SPHINX

There are plenty of deserts in Minecraft, and even the odd temple, but as fun as it is to build pyramids, your Egyptian-style monuments won't be complete without a Sphinx! It will look purr-fect!

PUZZLE PAGES

Can you spot the six changes we've made to the picture?

SPOT THE DIFFERENCE

MINECRAFTIFY

Can you name the nine delicious foods we've treated
to a Minecraft makeover?

Looking for inspiration? Check out our huge collection of YouTubers and builds!

WEBSITES & YOUTUBERS!

YOUTUBERS

DanTDM
We couldn't leave out DanTDM when namechecking the best YouTubers around. He posts fewer Minecraft videos these days, but he still checks in with the community and goes on hilarious adventures with Doctor Trayaurus, who has almost become more of a well-known character than Dan at this point! With over 21 million subscribers now, Dan is simply unstoppable.
tinyurl.com/MC2020YT1

Mini Muka
If roleplay videos are your thing, then get ready to have some serious Minecraft fun with Muka!

Not only are his roleplay adventures epic, he does loads of live videos too. From making a secret base to running Noob Vs Pro diamond races, there will definitely be something to eat up your time on Muka's channel.
tinyurl.com/MC2020YT2

Preston
Preston is still posting the odd Minecraft video or two and they're always worth a look. Many of the more recent ones end up with him trolling his little brother, but to be fair the little guy does keep coming back for more! Preston's channel is all about getting the most fun possible out of games, Minecraft included!
tinyurl.com/MC2020YT3

CaptainSparklez
One of the biggest Minecraft YouTubers, CaptainSparklez is still going strong, making Minecraft music videos to pair with his own songs, and delighting just about everyone while doing it. Plenty of tips, tricks and extras are stuffed in-between the musical madness, so you'll not go wrong subscribing to this one!
tinyurl.com/MC2020YT4

MagmaMusen
MagmaMusen is a growing fave on YouTube, and it's not hard to see why. His family-friendly tutorials are easy to follow and tackle just about every little thing you could want to accomplish in Minecraft.

Want to make a DJ booth? Want to make a bubble bath? Want to make a goat? Yes, a goat! MagmaMusen is your one-stop tutorial shop. **tinyurl.com/MC2020YT5**

Netty Plays

Indeed! Netty plays! Mainly Minecraft minigames and survival. She's just so watchable and easy to spend time with, which is good because she's one of the top live Minecraft queens of YouTube. Accompany Netty on the highs and lows of her adventures, and have fun playing minigames in real time with one of the loveliest in the biz. **tinyurl.com/MC2020YT6**

Lextube

Minecraft Mods, Minecraft Let's Build, Timelapses, Modded Minecraft and more besides. Phew! Lextube tries to update seven days a week, so you'll always find something new and interesting to discover on his ever-popular channel. UK players will be overjoyed to see plenty of videos tailored to local interests here too. **tinyurl.com/MC2020YT7**

Baby Duck

Baby Duck likes cookies. Oh, also Minecraft! If you want cookies, you're reading the wrong book. No recipes here. If you want crazy adventures, Baby Duck has

it covered. Evil grannies, spooky vampire lairs and superheroes gone wrong, there's rarely a scenario that hasn't made the cut. There's always an evil "something" on the loose! **tinyurl.com/MC2020YT8**

PixelDip

Really going the extra mile to weave wonderful stories with Minecraft, PixelDip doesn't upload videos as often as a lot of other YouTubers, but you know that when one pops up it's going to be worth the wait. Featuring story-based Minecraft videos to inspire and intrigue you, PixelDip will take you on adventures you never dreamed possible. **tinyurl.com/MC2020YT9**

LDShadowLady

With around 5 million subscribers, Lizzie's Minecraft series are the ones to beat. Using mods like Minecraft One Life, Ultra Hardcore, Base Invaders and Shadowcraft, she always has something to reel you in. Once you've watched a few of her vids, it will be easy to see why she's one of the most incredible YouTubers around. **tinyurl.com/ MC2020YT10**

BUILDS

Rose

Sometimes the simplest things keep us happy, and this beautiful rose is so sweet we can practically smell it. The creator built it as a test, and it only took a couple of hours using the Arceon Loft tool! Wonderful. Now, can we have a dozen, please? **tinyurl.com/MC2020B10**

Buried Skeleton

Not much to do here except marvel in the magnificence of this enormous skeleton built into the earth like a giant, extinct humanoid alien creature that failed to survive an apocalyptic event. The crater terrain was constructed in World Machine, and the skeleton was made with the OMB plugin. **tinyurl.com/MC2020B9**

Roses are red

One of the best ways to protect your base is to make sure no one even knows it's there – and to do that, you'll have to make a secret entrance! Here are a few ways you can do it...

HOW TO MAKE A SECRET

A tree entrance with its cover ferns removed

An underwater tunnel

HIDDEN TREE ENTRANCE

If you're in a biome with larger trees, you can easily hide a doorway inside one! This is a little harder to do if the trees are slim, but dark oak and jungle trees are great for it! All you have to do is make the trunk three blocks wide and three blocks deep, then cut a hole in the middle, with a pit directly under the centre.

Now, add a door of whatever type blends into the wood best. You can further obscure its appearance by adding a thicket of flower bushes, large ferns, tall grass or whatever plant is common to the biome you're in!

UNDERWATER TUNNEL

If your base is near to deep water, you can add an underwater tunnel where you can get in and out without others finding it. The secret here is to make sure you can't see the entrance when you're on the surface of the water. The easiest way to

An uncovered waterfall entrance

ENTRANCE

A painting from the inside

do this is to build a pipe jutting outwards, then make it so you can swim into it from below. Once the tunnel is built, make sure no light leaks out, and camouflage the top.

WATERFALL ENTRANCE

There are caves everywhere in Minecraft, and it's not unusual to see water springing from a mountainside. You can use these two facts to create a secret door to your base! Either find an existing water spring

Vines obscure an entrance

or embed a water source block above the place you want to make your entrance, then carve a small hole in the rock behind where it's flowing, ideally some way up the mountainside. If you do it correctly, the water will make it hard to see the entrance, then when you want to use it you can swim up the downward flowing water and slip inside your base without anyone realising!

INVISIBLE DOORWAY

The simplest of secret entrances: build an S-shaped passage into a hill near your base. The bend will make it impossible to see the door from the outside no matter what angle you're looking at it from. The larger you make the passage,

the easier it will be to hide, and it can help to put vines, tall plants or sugar cane in front so it's even harder to make out. Again, keep light sources far away!

PAINTING DOOR

A fairly simple but impressive secret door: craft a 2x1 tunnel, then place two signs, one on top of the other, in the space. Place a painting on the wall to the bottom left of the passage and it will cover up the whole thing (assuming there's space). You can then run in and out without anyone else knowing that's how you did it. Genius!

Diamond ore

Straight acacia tree trunk

Bed

RARE PLANTS AND BLOCKS

10 points each

53 Diamond ore
54 Any loot chest
55 Packed ice
56 Acacia tree with a completely straight trunk
57 Small jungle tree
58 Sponge blocks
59 Carved sandstone
60 Bed
61 Banner

SUPER-RARE PLANTS AND BLOCKS

20 points each

62 Bone blocks (found as part of a fossil)
63 Damaged anvil (hint: search woodland mansions)
64 Blue ice
65 Tree whose leaves are discoloured from crossing biomes
66 Tall birch tree
67 Blocks of gold
68 Glazed terracotta

Bone blocks

Blue ice

Blocks of gold

THE COMPLETE LOOT AND TREASURE GUIDE

Minecraft is full of riches, often found in chests dotted around the world! If you're after something specific, learn where to search!

All of these item lists are ordered from the most common to the most rare. Remember that chests contain a random selection of items from the lists given, not EVERYTHING! While there is some crossover in the items you can find, some chests have items that can't be found in other types of chest, so watch out for those!

BONUS CHESTS

A bonus chest is generated at the spawn point if you tick the box during world generation. It contains loot that's useful early on: sticks, oak planks, apples, raw salmon, bread, wooden pickaxe, wooden axe, spruce log, oak log, jungle log, dark oak log, birch log, acacia log, stone pickaxe and stone axe.

BURIED TREASURE

Buried treasure can be found under the sea floor using maps or by following friendly dolphins. They contain super-valuable items: iron ingots, gold ingots, emeralds, cooked salmon, cooked cod, prismarine crystals, TNT, diamonds, a heart of the sea, iron swords and leather tunics.

IGLOOS

If an igloo has a hidden basement, you'll find a chest containing any of coal, apples, wheat, gold nuggets, golden apples, rotten flesh, stone axes and emeralds.

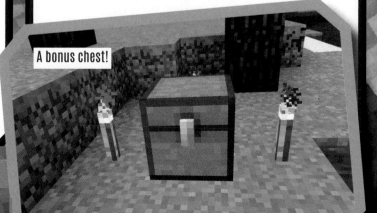

A bonus chest!

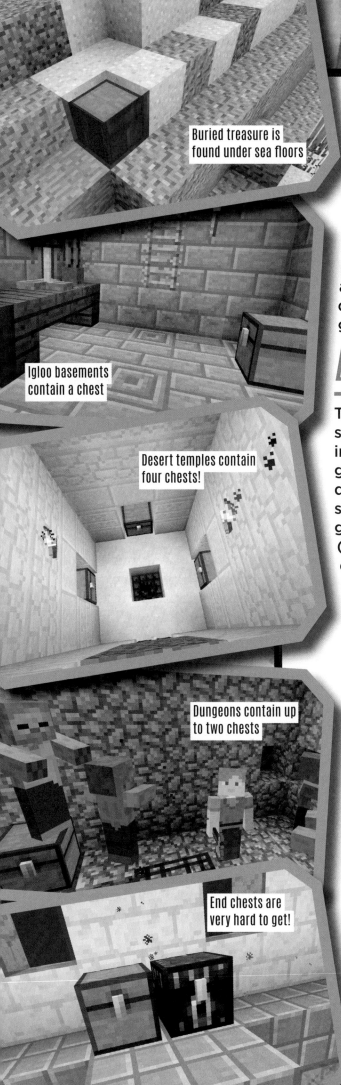

Buried treasure is found under sea floors

Igloo basements contain a chest

Desert temples contain four chests!

Dungeons contain up to two chests

End chests are very hard to get!

DESERT TEMPLES

If you find a desert temple, you're in luck as they contain four chests! The loot isn't very unique, but at least there's a lot of it! Each chest can contain bones, rotten flesh, gunpowder, sand, string, gold ingots, spider eyes, iron ingots, emeralds, enchanted books, saddles, golden apples, iron horse armour, golden horse armour, diamonds, diamond horse armour and enchanted golden apples.

DUNGEONS

These small chambers containing monster spawners can have up to two chests. The loot inside is a selection of bones, rotten flesh, gunpowder, string, wheat, coal, redstone dust, beetroot seeds, melon seeds, pumpkin seeds, iron ingots, bread, name tags, saddles, gold ingots, golden apples, music discs ("13" or "Cat"), buckets, iron horse armour, enchanted books, gold horse armour, diamond horse armour and enchanted golden apples.

END CITIES

The chests in End cities are very hard to get to and only accessible very late in the game, so they have the best loot by far. You can expect to see gold ingots, iron ingots, beetroot seeds, diamonds, emeralds, enchanted diamond armour (all pieces), enchanted diamond pickaxes, shovels and swords, enchanted iron armour (all pieces), enchanted iron pickaxes, shovels and swords, saddles, iron horse armour, golden horse armour and diamond horse armour.

The enchantments on enchanted items are usually very high – the same as you'd receive for a Level 39 enchantment, which is higher than it's possible to even make using an enchantment table (they're capped at Level 30!).

Jungle temple have visible and hidden chests

Look out for abandoned chest minecarts

Shipwrecks have three types of chest

Ruins have large or small chests

JUNGLE TEMPLES

Jungle temples have two chests: one visible, one hidden. The loot in both contains bones, rotten flesh, gold ingots, iron ingots, diamonds, emeralds, saddles, iron horse armour, gold horse armour, diamond horse armour and enchanted books.

ABANDONED MINES

In abandoned mines, you'll occasionally find abandoned chest minecarts. These act the same as normal treasure chests and contain torches, rails, coal, lapis lazuli, redstone, bread, iron ingots, beetroot seeds, melon seeds, pumpkin seeds, activator rails, detector rails, powered rails, name tags, gold ingots, golden apples, diamonds, enchanted books, iron pickaxes and enchanted golden apples.

SHIPWRECKS

There are three types of chest in a shipwreck: **Map chests** contain paper, feathers, books, buried treasure maps, empty maps, compasses and clocks.

Supply chests contain wheat, rotten flesh, paper, carrot, coal, potato, poisonous potato, gunpowder, pumpkin, enchanted leather clothes (all pieces) and TNT.

Treasure chests contain iron nuggets, iron ingots, lapis lazuli, emerald, gold nuggets, gold ingots, bottle o' enchanting and diamonds.

RUINS

Underwater ruins have two variants depending on whether the ruin is large or small. Large ones contain coal, wheat, gold nuggets, buried treasure maps, enchanted books, enchanted fishing rods, emeralds, golden apples, golden helmets and leather tunics. Small ones don't have gold items or enchanted books, and instead contain rotten flesh and a stone axe.

NETHER FORTRESSES

Chests in the Nether have lots of great loot, which is no surprise given how hard it is to get it home safely! You can find gold ingots, Nether wart, iron ingots, diamonds, saddles, gold horse armour, obsidian, iron horse armour, flint and steel, golden chestplate, golden sword and diamond horse armour.

Nether fortress chests contain cool loot!

Strongholds contain a lot of chests!

STRONGHOLDS

The size of strongholds means there are lots of items to find and three different types of chest, depending on the rooms in the stronghold. You can expect to find a good number of chests in any stronghold you visit!

Altar chests contain redstone, bread, iron ingots, apples, gold ingots, ender pearls, diamonds, iron pickaxes, iron armour (all pieces), iron swords, golden apples, saddles, diamond horse armour, gold horse armour, iron horse armour and enchanted books.

In libraries, the chests contain just a few items, but they're very uncommon: paper, books, enchanted books, compasses and empty maps.

Finally, storeroom chests can contain coal, redstone, bread, iron ingots, apples, gold ingots, enchanted books and iron pickaxes.

WOODLAND MANSIONS

These huge, mysterious buildings can contain chests in a number of spots, but each one has the same chance of containing the same items: gunpowder, string, bone, rotten flesh, wheat, coal, redstone dust, pumpkin seeds, melon seeds, beetroot seeds, iron ingots, bread, leads, name tags, gold ingots, diamond hoes, music discs ("Cat" and "13"), golden apples, buckets, chainmail chestplate, enchanted books, diamond chestplates and enchanted golden apples.

Woodland mansions contain a number of chests

It you want to create an amazing Minecraft build, it makes sense to take a bit of time planning it first! It's worth sketching out your idea and finding any problems before you head to the game. Plus, if you have something to refer to, it tends to make things easier!

PLANNING A BRILLIANT MINECRAFT BUILD!

On the right, you'll find a sheet of planning paper for you to draw your build on. But before you get out your pencils, consider the following:

☐ Is it just your building, or are you working with friends/siblings? If others are involved, make them part of the planning process, then divide up the work between you!

☐ Start small! If it's one of your first builds, focus on building a small house and on making it as brilliant as possible.

☐ Do the edges and the corners first! Then you can gradually fill in your build from the outside in.

☐ Save the details for later! For now, just get the basic structure in place. You can decorate it once you've finished!

☐ Don't be afraid to rub it all out and start again! Sometimes a good idea just doesn't work out. It happens to us all and is part of the fun of putting together a Minecraft build!

FURNITURE MINI-BUILDS

Kitting out your base is always a fun way to spend time, so here are a few of our favourite furniture mini-builds to give you that polished look in minutes!

Relax after a busy day...

Impress with this clock

BATHTUB

You need: **Trapdoors, buckets of water, tripwire hooks**
Place the trapdoors (birch ones look best, but you can use any kind) on the floor, then open them so they stand up to create the edge of the bath. Fill the inside with water and use tripwire hooks as "taps".

GRANDFATHER CLOCK

You need: **Dark oak bark, item frames, shovel, stick, clock**
Use bark blocks to build a tall post, then, using item frames, attach a clock face to the top. Put a stick in the middle and a shovel below to look like a pendulum – you'll have to rotate them both to line up!

FIREPLACE

You need: **Slabs, iron bars, paintings, plant pots, flowers, Netherrack, flint and steel**
A fireplace will brighten up any room. Use slabs to build the frame, and place railings in front as a fire guard. Netherrack burns forever, so use that as the "fuel"!

Create a cosy look

Add a pop of colour!

CURTAINS

You need: Banners
Fairly simple: just attach two banners to the top of a window to create a pair of curtains – they'll attach to glass panes without any problem!

Create some mood lighting

FLOOR LAMP

You need: End rods, plant pot
Stack two End rods on top of each other, then put a plant pot on the top to look like a lampshade. The End rods will be emitting the light, but it looks like a free-standing floor lamp!

DESK LAMP

You need: Sea lantern, trapdoors, fence post
Surround a sea lantern (or any glowing block) with trapdoors (except on the bottom) and place a fence post underneath to create a desk lamp.

Place it on your desk...

Just need a coffee table now

SOFA

You need: Stairs, trapdoors
To make a sofa, put two stair blocks next to one another, then put trapdoors at either end so that when you open them they sit alongside the blocks to form armrests.

Loads of room for two!

...next to your computer

COMPUTER

You need: Stairs, activator rail, painting
Stick a painting to the back of any stair block to act as the screen, and an activator rail in front to be the "keyboard".

Make your room look more alive

DOUBLE BED

You need: Any two beds
There's no secret to this one – to make a double-sized bed, you can easily place two beds right next to one another and they'll look perfect.

PLANTER

You need: Dirt, trapdoors, a plant
Surround a dirt block with trapdoors, then open them to create a large wooden planter. Now put in your plant!

OUTDOOR
MINI-BUILDS

Filled your base and want to start landscaping the world around it? Here are a few more mini-builds to make your world look awesome without taking forever to craft!

GRAVE

You need: Sign, polished andesite, torch, chests
Dig two blocks down and two across, and place a double chest in the open pit for a "coffin". Cover it with andesite, then use another andesite block with a torch and sign attached as the headstone. You can write anyone's name you like.

In Memory of Solarax

Spooooky!

HOT TUB

You need: Lava, water, glass blocks, stairs, levers
Dig down two blocks and place some lava blocks in the bottom of your pit. Cover them with glass blocks to make a see-through floor, then surround that with stairs. Fill the inside with water, then attach levers nearby to look like water taps. Voilà: one heated pool!

PATIO SET

You need: Quartz stairs, carpet, fence posts, sandstone, slabs
Make your furniture white to resemble garden furniture. A checkerboard pattern made using sandstone and stone slabs will look better than a single design on its own.

Anyone for a quick dip?

OLD WELL

You need: Mossy cobblestone wall, cobblestone wall, cobblestone stairs, iron bar, mossy cobblestone, water

Dig a deep pit one block wide, then line the edge with mossy cobblestone. Fill it with water, then put a mossy wall around it. Use wall posts at each corner to support the "roof" made of stairs. Finally, hang an iron bar from the centre to look like a bucket lowering in.

Perfect for a medieval village build

SPOOKY GATES

You need: Iron bars, spruce doors, torches, stone blocks

Building gates this way, with high gateposts and iron railings, makes them look more imposing – perfect for graveyards, haunted houses or old mansions.

MARKET

You need: Oak logs, stairs, oak planks, chests

Why not create a small market-style shop? Build a frame using oak, then add a roof and a back wall. Put counters alongside chests for shoppers to browse. Display cakes, plants, or any other placeable item.

These are pretty impressive gates

STATUE

You need: Slabs, armour, armour stand, mob head

Build a plinth using slabs, put an armour stand on top, then hang the armour and head on the stand. You can swap one of the slabs for a sign if you want space to explain who the statue is!

Who would you have as a statue?

SEWER

You need: Ladder, trapdoor, mossy stone bricks

Carve out the area under your streets to build a network of sewers! Use just one source block so the water looks like it's flowing, and mossy stone bricks for that damp look. Use a ladder with a trapdoor for a manhole cover.

PARK

You need: Gravel, flowers, lily pads, stairs, iron bars, water, tree

Fence off an area using iron bars as railings, then add a gravel path. Put in a pond and stairs for a bench, then decorate with flowers and a tree. Now you can relax in your own park!

PUZZLE PAGES

Can you spot the seven changes we've made to the picture?

SPOT THE DIFFERENCE

BLOCK MAZE

Can you find the centre of our maze and bag the emerald?

Start here!

10 GAMES TO PLAY IN MULTIPLAYER MODE

Want to play AGAINST your pals rather than alongside them? Here are 10 competition-style minigames! Set the game to Peaceful for the best results.

DEATHMATCH

The only rule here is the last one standing wins! It's a group fight to the death, where only one person can succeed. Keep your inventory safe in a chest!

TAG

Set a time limit and fence off an area, then keep track of who's "it". Whoever's tagged when the time limit runs out loses, and the next round continues without them.

HIDE & SEEK

Agree on a place to hide (this is good fun in villages and mansions!), then one player has to try to find the others. You could also do it so that players who are found join in the search, to make the game shorter and more fun!

Invite other players to deathmatch with them

CAPTURE THE FLAG

Divide your group into two teams, each with their own single banner. Your goal is to capture the opponent's banner and bring it home while protecting your own! Hint: keep some spares in case your flag is destroyed or lost.

Shhhh, keep hidden

TARGET PRACTICE

Build a circular target 50 blocks away using coloured blocks – it can be upright or on the ground – then take turns firing three arrows from the 50-block line to see who can get them closest to the bullseye.

BOXING

Craft a small arena, drop all your weapons, armour and other combat items, then fight to the death using only your melee fists. The secret is to dodge and weave while going on the offensive.

FOOTRACE

Choose a landmark far away in the distance and see who can reach it first. Try to take different routes, otherwise it won't be as much fun! Boats, horses and vehicles are not allowed!

Capturing the flag is only half the fight!

SWIMMING RACE

Unlike walking, it takes skill to swim properly in Minecraft, so why not have a race across a lake or ocean? Manage your oxygen, avoid threats, or get a speed boost from a dolphin!

HIGH DIVE

Build a high dive board and jump off into a pool below. Next go, make the pool a bit smaller, and see if you can make it again. Repeat until the target is a single block of water or everyone loses their life...

Build a target!

Put your fists up

SCAVENGER RACE

A scavenger hunt where one person chooses a block type and every other player has to run out and find it. The last person to return with the block (or item) picks next time.

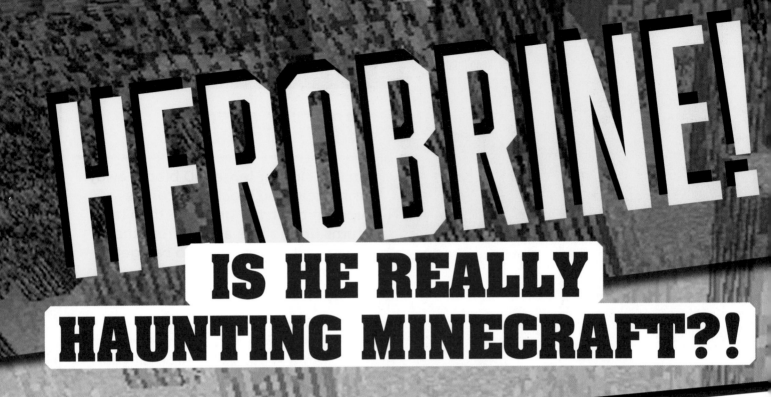

HEROBRINE!

IS HE REALLY HAUNTING MINECRAFT?!

Minecraft has its very own ghost – or does it?!

For years, Minecraft players the world over have been divided about Herobrine. Does he exist? Is he real? Well, the makers of the game insist he's not. But many disagree!

The first reported sighting was in the early days of the game. A player reported chopping up some wood on the PC version.

Their PC wasn't very good, though, so its graphics settings weren't very high. Still, the player reckoned they saw a figure moving in the fog, and duly gave chase. They thought it was Steve – but was it? It was a character with a Steve skin, certainly, but with no name above his head. And instead of eyes, there was nothing!

Excitedly, the player tried to post about what they'd seen, but reckoned their post kept getting deleted. Then they said they got a message from a player going by the name of Herobrine. The message simply said: "Stop"!

Did all this happen? Who knows. But the mystery soon deepened! Claims were made that Herobrine was the brother of Minecraft creator, Notch. He denied this, saying Herobrine wasn't real.

So who is this mysterious guy?

Could this REALLY be him?

WHAT DOES HEROBRINE DO?
Apparently, Herobrine has been known to...

☐ Create odd and random things, such as long 2x2 tunnels
☐ Cut leaves off trees
☐ Run, but he can't fly
☐ Take control of passive mobs, and sometimes revive undead mobs!

Evidence of Herobrine or not?

But the reports kept coming. Some were easy to dismisses as hoaxes, from people messing around with graphics software. But could they all be fake? On a live stream by a player called Copeland, there was said to be a sighting of Herobrine in a house. Another user, Patimuss, reckoned they met him in a live stream, in the middle of a lava field! Readers of *Minecraft World* magazine regularly write in and say they've seen him too.

But is he real? Well, going back to those two streams – from Copeland and Patimuss – they were eventually revealed to be fakes. The people behind Minecraft have always argued that Herobrine has never been part of the game. They occasionally write for a joke "Herobrine removed" when releasing notes for Minecraft updates. And Herobrine has popped up in a banner advertising an official Minecraft convention.

Still, people have gone through the programming code for the game and found no reference at all to him.

Why, then, do people keep seeing him? There are regular claims that Herobrine has been seen, and some people have even built tributes to him.

What do YOU think? Is Herobrine real?!

YES ☐   NO ☐

I had recently spawned a new world in single-player Minecraft. Everything was normal at first as I began chopping down trees and crafting a workbench. I noticed something move amongst the dense fog (I have a very slow computer so I have to play with tiny render distance). I thought it was a cow, so I pursued it, hoping to grab some hides for armor.

It wasn't a cow though. Looking back at me was another character with the default skin, but his eyes were empty. I saw no name pop-up, and I double-checked to make sure I wasn't in multiplayer mode. He didn't stay long, he looked at me and quickly ran into the fog. I pursued out of curiousity, but he was gone.

I continued on with the game, not sure what to think. As I expanded the world I saw things that seemed out of place for the random map generator to make; 2x2 tunnels in the rocks, small perfect pyramids made of sand in the ocean, and groves of trees with all their leaves cut off. I would constantly think I saw the other "player" in the deep fog, but I never got a better look at him. I tried increasing my render distance to far whenever I thought I saw him, but to no avail.

I saved the map and went on to the forums to see if anyone else had found the pseudo-player. There were none. I created my own topic telling of the man and asking if anyone had a similar experience. The post was deleted within five minutes. I tried again, and the topic was deleted even faster. I recieved a PM from username 'Herobrine' containing one word: 'Stop.' When I went to look at Herobrine's profile, the page 404'd.

I recieved an email from another forum user. He claimed the mods can read the forum user messages, so we were safer using email. The emailer claimed that he had seen the mystery player too, and had a small 'directory' of other users who had seen him as well. Their worlds were littered with obviously man-made features as well, and described their mystery player to have no pupils.

About a month passed until I heard from my informant again. Some of the people who had encountered the mystery man had looked into the name Herobrine and found that name to be frequently used by a swedish gamer. After some further information gathering, it was revealed to be the brother of Notch, the game's developer. I personally emailed Notch, and asked him if he had a brother. It took him a while, but he emailed me back a very short message.

'I did, but he is no longer with us.'
-Notch

I haven't seen the mystery man since our first encounter, and I haven't noticed any changes to the world other than my own. I was able to press 'print screen' when I first saw him. Here's the only evidence I have of his existence.

Minecraft Alpha v1.8.16_92

The first sighting?

53

SCAVENGER HUNT PART 3

You've reached Part 3 of our giant scavenger hunt! Can you track down and take a screenshot of EVERYTHING on our list? There are 101 items to find spread across the annual – here are the final 33! This time, they're themed on the Nether and the End. Remember they have to be NATURALLY generated – stuff you craft or place doesn't count!

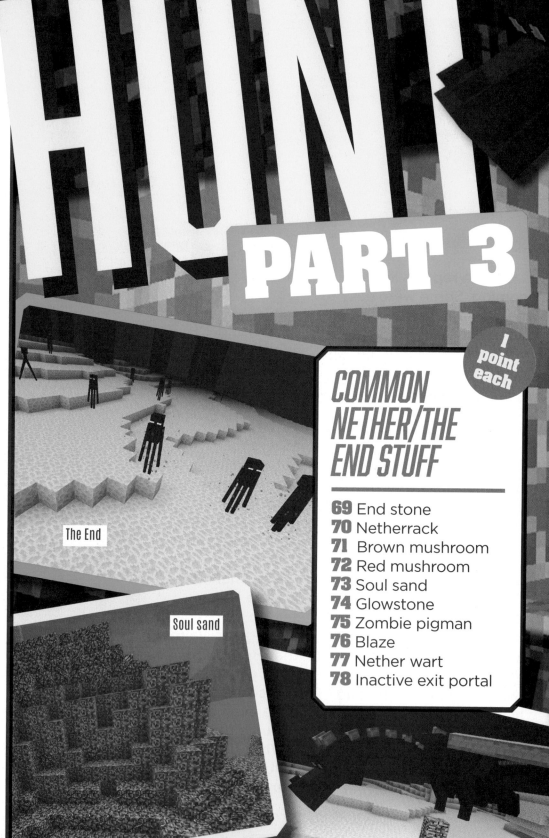

The End

Soul sand

COMMON NETHER/THE END STUFF

1 point each

69 End stone
70 Netherrack
71 Brown mushroom
72 Red mushroom
73 Soul sand
74 Glowstone
75 Zombie pigman
76 Blaze
77 Nether wart
78 Inactive exit portal

An inactive portal

LESS COMMON NETHER/THE END STUFF

5 points each

79 Iron railings
80 Chorus plant
81 Gravel
82 Nether quartz ore
83 Ghast
84 Wither skeleton
85 Bedrock
86 Nether bricks

Chorus plants

Nether bedrock

A ghast. Terrifying!

Purpur blocks

Magma blocks

End rods

RARE NETHER/ THE END STUFF

10 points each

87 Purpur blocks
88 Purpur pillars
89 End stone bricks
90 Magma blocks
91 Endermen
92 (Non-wither) skeleton
93 Loot chest
94 End rods

SUPER-RARE NETHER/THE END STUFF

20 points each

95 Dragon's head
96 Elytra in an item frame
97 Mob spawner
98 Magma cubes
99 Active exit portal
100 Purple and black banners
101 Purple stained glass blocks

A dragon head

Elytra in a frame

An active portal

NIGHT SECRETS

When night falls, the Overworld changes in more ways than just how light it is. Here are all the things you need to know about Minecraft's darkest hours...

Sunset in Minecraft

LIGHT LEVELS

When the sun sets completely, the light level across the entire world is set to 4, which means hostile mobs can spawn anywhere on the surface of the Overworld. Mobs can only spawn where the light level is less than 7, which is why torches and lamps are important for keeping them away at night.

Mobs spawn at night

NIGHT TIME

It takes 20 minutes for the entire day-night cycle to run in Minecraft. Daytime lasts for 10 minutes, Sunset and Sunrise last for 90 seconds each, and the dangerous, mob-spawning part of night runs for seven minutes.

A NEW PHASE

The moon is only visible at night, and changes phase with every night-day cycle. Like in real life, there are eight moon phases, which run in a repeating pattern. The phase of the moon has a number of effects on how mobs behave. Usually, the fuller the moon, the bigger its effect on mobs, but it also depends on other factors, such as game difficulty. When the moon is full, more slimes will spawn in swamp biomes, and more mobs can spawn with status effects, armour and weapon enchantments that make them harder to kill.

The moon can affect mobs

SLEEP TIGHT

One of the best ways to deal with night is to simply sleep through it! If you make a bed, you can sleep in it once night begins and skip the dangerous hours completely. But while this is a convenient way to avoid mobs, you should remember that when you sleep in a bed, your game essentially pauses. Your crops won't grow, your furnaces won't smelt or cook, even water and lava will stop flowing.

Sleep through the night!

A RAINY DAY

There's only one time you can sleep in a bed when it isn't night, and that's during a storm. When you wake up, the storm will have passed and the rain will be gone, so it's a good way to stop lightning damaging buildings!

Sleep in your beds at the same time!

Use the moon as a compass

SLEEPOVER TIME!

If you're playing a multiplayer game, remember all players must sleep in their beds at the same time to skip the night. You can't sleep in a bed already occupied by another player, so everyone needs to get in their own before the night will advance! Co-ordinate this in the chat console.

STAR CHARTS

At night, the moon and stars travel in the same direction as Minecraft's Sun: east to west. If you don't have a compass or map, you can use the moon to navigate. If the moon is rising, walking towards it means you're going east. If the moon is setting, walking towards it means you're travelling west.

THE END SECRETS

Of all the dimensions you can travel around in Minecraft, the End is the most mysterious. But don't get confused or intimidated by its strange landscape and weird mobs – here's all the cool stuff you need to know...

Don't fall into the Void!

ISLAND HOPPING

When you first enter the End, you'll arrive on the large central island. This island is surrounded (at a huge distance) by lots of other islands, some large, some small. They all float in the Void, which is a never-ending world of empty space. If you fall into the Void, there's no way back! Instead, to travel between islands, you should use ender pearls collected from endermen. Throw a pearl and you'll teleport to where it lands. Just don't miss when you throw it!

DRAGON PUNCH

The ender dragon lives on the central island and never leaves it. You can travel to (and later back from) the outer islands by throwing an ender pearl into an End gateway, but they only appear after the dragon has been defeated. The exit portal, which is made of indestructible bedrock, is also found on the central island. It leads back to the Overworld, but also only activates once the dragon is dead.

Chorus trees planted in End stone

UNEXPECTED END

Although lots of things work the same in the End as in the Overworld, there are a few major exceptions. Maps work in the End, but compasses are no help and spin randomly. Similarly, beds explode if placed in the End, so don't even try! There is one good thing, though: the End has its own unique music soundtrack!

CHORUS LINE

Chorus plants (sometimes called chorus trees) are strange, tall purple plants that only grow if planted in End stone. Fully grown plants have chorus flowers on the end of their branches, which drop chorus fruit when broken by the player. Chorus fruit can be popped in a furnace, then crafted into purpur blocks.

SHULKAMANIA

Shulkers are mobs that live in End cities and disguise themselves as blocks similar to purpur. They have 20 armour points when closed, and will teleport to safety if attacked. Killing one will drop 5 experience and 0-1 shulker shells. Two shells can be crafted with a chest into a shulker box, which can carry items as additional inventory space and also be dyed any colour. Their attacks inflict the Levitation effect, so take care!

The ender dragon lives on the central island

STRANGE FRUIT

Be careful when eating a popped chorus fruit. As well as offering a small health boost, they teleport you a short distance, so don't eat one too close to the edge of an island, otherwise you could plummet into the Void. They're the only way to get back health and sate hunger in the End, though!

END LOOT

Chests in End cities have by far the best loot, with lots of enchanted tools and armour, but watch out for cities with End ships. As well as having the rare dragon head block as their figurehead, they contain the rare and super-fun elytra item, which allows you to glide long distances when worn!

THE NETHER SECRETS

The Nether is a terrifying and hostile dimension, but if you want to access the game's best enchantments and potions you'll have to visit sometime. And when you do, here are the things you'll want to remember to make it as easy as possible!

Make mushroom stew!

Time pauses in the Overworld

IN A STEW

The Nether doesn't have many sources of food, so make sure you have a bowl with you in case you run out. There are tonnes of mushrooms in the Nether, meaning you can craft mushroom stew out of one red and one brown mushroom. You CAN grow other plants in the Nether if you import dirt from the Overworld, but most crops can't grow, as water evaporates immediately.

NETHER SAY NETHER AGAIN

In single player mode, entering the Nether will essentially pause time in the Overworld – crops won't grow, fires won't spread, furnaces won't continue smelting, and mobs will remain in place until you return!

SAND HASSLE

Soul sand slows down any player or mob that walks on it, so try not to do it! If you bring it to the Overworld and place it underwater, it will form a column of bubbles that pushes upwards anything that swims into it. Magma blocks, which can also be found in the Nether, do the opposite – they pull things down underwater.

Soul sand will slow you down

FORT-RIGHT

Nether fortresses are the only place in the Nether you can find chests, and they're full of useful loot, which is no surprise given how hard it is to get it home safely! The most useful thing about Nether fortress chests is they can contain everything you need to build a portal back to the Overworld!

LONG-DISTANCE WALKING

When you're in the Nether, every block's distance you travel is worth eight in the Overworld. So if you enter the Nether, travel very far, then build a Nether portal to return to the Overworld you'll be eight times further away – if you can survive that long!

Use the Nether to travel long distances

NETHER MIND THE MOBS

The Nether is full of mobs, but they behave differently in certain areas. Ghasts don't spawn in and around Nether fortresses, zombie pigmen are rarer in fortresses than outside, while blazes and wither skeletons only spawn inside fortresses. In general, mobs spawn faster in Nether fortresses than outside, so you'll never clear them for long!

Nether fortresses can contain useful chests!

RACK 'EM UP

The most common block in the Nether is Netherrack. If you set it on fire, it will burn forever, so you can use it to make fireplaces or impressive-looking furnaces in the Overworld. Even rain doesn't put out fires if they're burning on Netherrack, though water will smother them. Netherrack can also be smelted to create Nether bricks, which can be crafted into blocks.

Minecraft's oceans are fuller than ever, and if you haven't explored the underwater features added in the last year, you're missing out on some amazing stuff. Here are our favourite secrets about the world beneath the waves...

UNDER

SUNKEN REMAINS

Ruins are the flooded remnants of villages from Minecraft's distant past. There are over 50 structure variants and you'll find them in the following biomes: Ocean, Cold Ocean, Frozen Ocean, Warm Ocean, Lukewarm Ocean, Deep Ocean, Deep Cold Ocean, Deep Frozen Ocean and Deep Lukewarm Ocean.

Purple terracotta can appear in ruins

NOT-SO-SUNKEN REMAINS

You can occasionally find ruins above ground – they can spawn on beaches, which makes them a lot easier to find and explore. You could even try rebuilding them!

Ruins are usually sunken...

TERRACOTTA ARMY

As of the Village & Pillage update, purple glazed terracotta appears in certain underwater ruins, and it's the only place you can find glazed terracotta. If you want to see another colour, you'll have to craft it!

...but can spawn above ground

WATER SECRETS

SWIM FOR YOUR LIFE

You can swim faster underwater by "sprinting" while submerged. When you're swimming (properly swimming, not just underwater), you can fit through 1x1 block gaps!

TURTLE-Y AWESOME

When a baby turtle grows into an adult, it drops a scute. You can craft five scutes into a turtle shell, and when worn as a helmet it will give you two extra armour points and 10 extra seconds of breath underwater.

OK CORAL

Coral blocks must be touching water to remain "alive" – if they're completely dry on all sides for a few seconds, the blocks will turn grey and become dead coral blocks. Once a coral block dies, there's no way to bring it back to life.

YOU CON-DU-IT!

Conduits are a bit like underwater beacons. Craft one from eight nautilus shells and one heart of the sea, then place it underwater. It allows you to breathe underwater, gives off a strong light, improves your underwater vision and increases underwater mining speed.

DOLPHIN-FRIENDLY

Dolphins will follow boats near the surface, and jump out of the water as they do. If you feed one a raw cod, it will lead you to the nearest buried treasure chest or shipwreck!

BEACH BABY

Turtles spawn on beaches and return to their "home" beach to lay eggs if they're ready to breed. Zombies and their variants will try to destroy the eggs, so protect them!

WATERCOLOURS

The colour of water indicates its temperature – the lighter the water, the warmer it is. If water is dark, it's harder to see through!

69

JOKES!

WHAT DID ALEX SAY WHEN SHE SAW HER HOUSE HAD BEEN FILLED WITH VEGETABLES?

There's not mush-room in here!

WHERE DID THE CREEPER FINISH IN THE RUNNING RACE?

In blast place!

WHY SHOULDN'T YOU TAKE THE ENDER DRAGON TO SEE A FILM?

Because he'll only be there for the end!

WHY WAS THERE A TRAFFIC JAM IN MINECRAFT?

Because of the road block!

KNOCK KNOCK! WHO'S THERE? THE INTERRUPTING CREEPER! THE INTERRUPTING CREE.... BOOOOOOOOOOOOOOOOOOOOOOOOM

Have you ever tried to survive on an island with virtually no chance of escape? Well, if not, now's your chance with our survival island challenge!

PART ONE: SETTING THE SCENE

Starting the challenge is simple: begin a new world where you start the game on an island surrounded by sea. You can use a pre-discovered seed or just keep trying out new seeds until you get an island. It's worth keeping a note of the seed you're using because you'll then be able to play the challenge against your friends and see who does it best!

The island can be any size and have any amount of resources on it, but here's the catch: you can only use what you find on the island to stay alive. That means food, resources and space are all limited. And how limited they are determines how difficult your challenge is...

Survival islands have few resources

This island has tonnes of trees!

A classic simple survival island

SURVIVAL ISLAND CHALLENGE

PART TWO: PICKING A CHALLENGE

There are lots of ways to play your survival island challenge. Here are some variants:

■ Survival Island Classic

For this challenge, all you have to do is stay alive. Sounds simple, right? Well, not when there's no food around! The goal is to live for as long as possible, which means feeding yourself well and protecting yourself against mobs. It's just like playing Minecraft, only you can't wander very far! Remember to count each morning – perhaps use the console to give yourself a book to write tally marks in, or come up with a counting system using blocks. The longer you live, the better!

■ Escape Challenge

We know we said you can't leave, but for this version of the challenge you're encouraged to! The trick here is that you have to do it quickly and you have to survive until you reach the mainland (which sounds easier than it is!). The easiest way is to build a boat, in which case you need to hope you don't get attacked on the way off the island. But you can also make the challenge a lot harder by agreeing that you have to build, dig or swim your way off!

■ Full Armour Challenge

With limited resources, how long will it take to build a full set of armour? Level 1 of the challenge is iron, Level 2 is gold, and Level 3 is diamond! This is great for multiplayer, where you can have a back-and-forth fight over the resources on a given island, where you don't have to just find the necessary materials – you also have to try and keep them safe!

■ Portal Challenge

If you can't escape the island in the Overworld, how about escaping to the Nether? This is a super-fun way to play a survival island where your only goal is to stay alive long enough to build a portal and disappear into the Nether. Extend the challenge by making your goal to reach the mainland through a return portal!

Could you escape?

It's tough to get to the Nether

Who knows what you'll find?!

THE BIG MINECRAFT QUIZ!

THE BIG MINECRAFT QUIZ!

Reckon you know your way around Minecraft? Take our quiz, and see how you measure up at the end!

1 IN WHAT YEAR WAS THE FIRST VERSION OF MINECRAFT OFFICIALLY RELEASED?

A 2005
B 2008
C 2011

2 WHICH OF THESE IS NOT A MOB IN MINECRAFT?

A Zombie pigman
B Turtle
C Owl

3 WHERE WILL YOU FIND THE ENDER DRAGON?

A The Start
B The Middle
C The End

4 WHAT DO YOU NEED TO POWER ITEMS IN MINECRAFT?

A Redstone
B Gas
C Wind

5 WITH WHICH OF THESE CAN YOU TRADE IN MINECRAFT?

A A skeleton
B A villager
C An ocelot

74

6 HOW BIG IS THE GRID IF YOU USE A CRAFTING TABLE TO CRAFT?
A 2x2
B 3x3
C 4x4

7 WHAT'S THE NAME OF THE ANNUAL ONLINE MINECRAFT CONVENTION?
A Minecon World
B Minecon Earth
C Minecon Global

8 WHICH OF THESE WAS AN ORIGINAL NAME FOR MINECRAFT?
A Blockbusters
B Cave Game
C Brickz

9 WHAT DO YOU NEED TO MAKE AN IRON GOLEM?
A Iron and pumpkin
B Iron and blue dye
C Iron and poisonous potato

10 WHICH OF THESE WAS THE NAME OF A MINECRAFT UPDATE?
A Update Gigantic
B Update Fantastic
C Update Aquatic

ANSWERS

1 C
2 C
3 C
4 A
5 B
6 B
7 B
8 B
9 A
10 C

HOW DID YOU DO?!

10: Wow! You're an absolute Minecraft expert. We're in awe!

8-9: You're an experienced Minecrafter and clearly know your way around the game!

6-7: You know lots about Minecraft, but we think there may still be a few things you don't know!

4-5: Not bad, but there's much in the world of Minecraft for you to discover!

0-3: Not to worry! You've now got a perfect excuse to learn even more about our favourite game!

ANSWERS

BLOCKDOKU (P14)

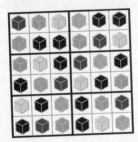
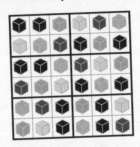
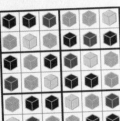
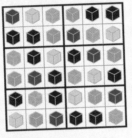
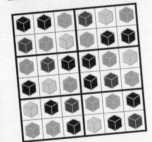
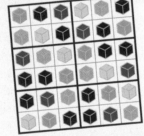
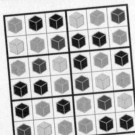
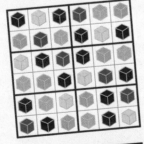
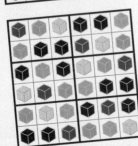
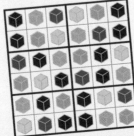

SPOT THE DIFFERENCE (P24)

BLOCKDOKU (P15)

MINECRAFTIFY(P25)

SPOT THE DIFFERENCE (P30)

WORDSEARCH (P31)

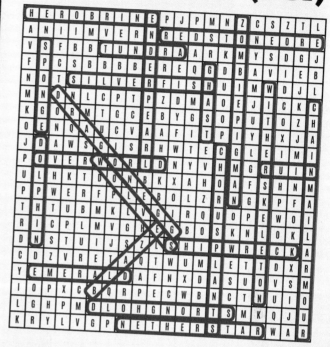

SPOT THE DIFFERENCE (P48)

BLOCK MAZE (P49)

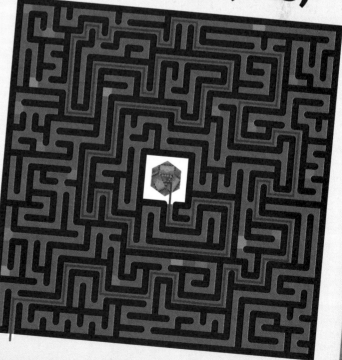

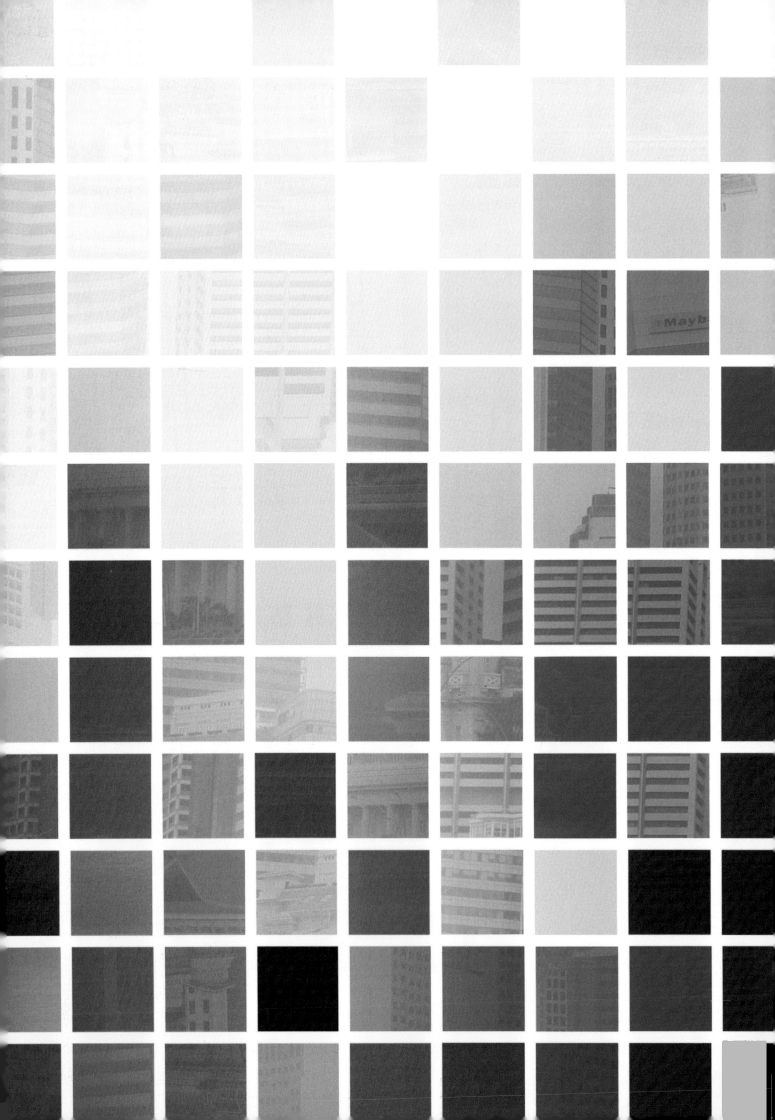